# HOW MANY DONKEYS?

## An Arabic Counting Tale

Retold from a Saudi folktale by

### Margaret Read MacDonald and Nadia Jameel Taibah

Illustrated by **Carol Liddiment**

**www.av2books.com**

## FICTION READALONG
### AV²
BY WEIGL™
ADDED VALUE • AUDIO VISUAL

Go to **www.av2books.com**,
and enter this book's
unique code.

**BOOK CODE**

**E 1 0 7 5 4 0**

AV² **by Weigl** brings you media
enhanced books that support
active learning.

First Published by

**ALBERT
WHITMAN
& COMPANY**
*Publishing children's books since 1919*

Your AV² Media Enhanced book gives you a fiction readalong online.
Log on to www.av2books.com and enter the unique book code from
this page to use your readalong.

# AV² Readalong Navigation

**HIGHLIGHTED TEXT**

**HOME** 🏠

**CLOSE** ⊗

**START READING**

**TITLE INFORMATION**

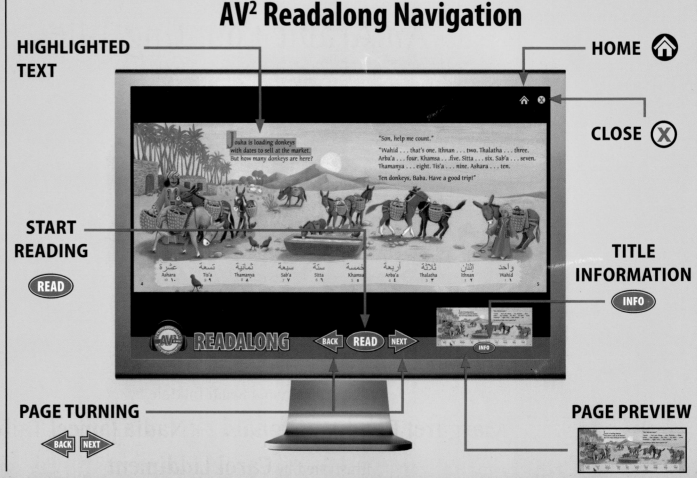

**PAGE TURNING**

**PAGE PREVIEW**

Published by AV² by Weigl
350 5th Avenue, 59th Floor New York, NY 10118

Copyright ©2013 AV² by Weigl

All rights reserved. No part of this publication may be reproduced, stored in a retrieval system, or transmitted in any form or by any means, electronic, mechanical, photocopying, recording, or otherwise, without the prior written permission of the publisher.
Printed in the United States of America in North Mankato, Minnesota

1 2 3 4 5 6 7 8 9 0    16 15 14 13 12

Text copyright © 2009 by Margaret Read MacDonald and Nadia Jameel Taibah. Illustrations copyright © 2009 by Carol Liddiment.
Published in 2009 by Albert Whitman & Company

052012
WEP160512

Library of Congress Cataloging-in-Publication Data

MacDonald, Margaret Read, 1940-

How many donkeys? : an Arabic counting tale / retold from a Saudi folktale by Margaret Read MacDonald and Nadia Jameel Taibah ; illustrated by Carol Liddiment.
  p. cm.

Summary: When Jouha counts the ten donkeys carrying his dates to market, he repeatedly forgets to count the one he is riding on, causing him great consternation. Includes numbers written out in Arabic and in English transliteration, as well as the numerals one through ten, and a note on the origins and other versions of the story.

Includes bibliographical references.

ISBN 978-1-61913-148-4 (hard cover : alk. paper)

[1. Arabs--Folklore. 2. Folklore--Arab countries. 3. Counting.]  I. Taibah, Nadia Jameel. II. Liddiment, Carol, ill. III. Title.
PZ8.1.M15924Ho 2012
398.20956--dc23
[E]

2012016793

Saudi storyteller Nadia Jameel Taibah heard this story from her aunt Salha.

Jouha (*JOU-huh*—ou as in *could*) is a wise fool much beloved in Middle Eastern folklore. These tales are told in Turkey about Nasr-din Hodja and in Iran about the Mullah. Egypt calls him Goha. Wherever he is found and under whatever name, his tales are always a mix of wisdom and foolishness, with trickster elements tossed in. In this book Jouha puts on his foolishness hat. Variants of this tale can be found in Nine in a Line by Ann Kirn (W. W. Norton, 1966) [Egypt], in Goha the Wise Fool by Denys Johnson-Davies (Philomel, 2005) [Egypt], and in *Once the Hodja* by Alice Kelsey (McKay, 1943) [Turkey].

The tale is found widely in folk literature under *Motif J2022 Numbskull cannot find ass he is sitting on. My Storyteller's Sourcebook* cites versions from Syria, Armenia, Turkey, and North Africa. The Iraqi dancer Farid Zodan recently told me a very similar Jouha tale well known in his family. Antti Aarne's The Types of the Folktale cites under Type 1288A variants from Spain, Germany, Italy, Hungary, Serbo-Croatia, and Puerto Rico. For a similar tale, *J2031 Counting wrong by not counting oneself,* Stith Thompson's *Motif-Index of Folk-Literature* cites tales from England, Turkey, Switzerland, India, and Indonesia. **M.R.M.**

Arabic is written from right to left, hence the order of the Arabic at the bottom of the pages. There are a variety of Arabic dialects. The pronunciations below are based on Modern Standard Arabic, which is the language of books and formal instruction used all over the Arabic world.

You can hear me say the numbers from one to ten on this web site: www.margaretreadmacdonald.com. **N.J.T.**

1 **Wahid**  wah HEHD (a as in *father*)

2 **Ithnan**  ihth NAHN

3 **Thalatha**  tha LA thuh (a as in *hat*)

4 **Arba'a**  AHR ba uh

5 **Khamsa**  KAHM suh

6 **Sitta**  SIHT tuh

7 **Sab'a**  SAHB uh

8 **Thamanya**  thah MAN ih yuh

9 **Tis'a**  TIHS uh

10 **Ashara**  AH shah rah

3

Jouha is loading donkeys
with dates to sell at the market.
But how many donkeys are here?

عشرة
Ashara
10 ١٠

تسعة
Tis'a
9 ٩

ثمانية
Thamanya
8 ٨

سبعة
Sab'a
7 ٧

ستة
Sitta
6 ٦

"Son, help me count."

"Wahid . . . that's one. Ithnan . . . two. Thalatha . . . three. Arba'a . . . four. Khamsa . . . five. Sitta . . . six. Sab'a . . . seven. Thamanya . . . eight. Tis'a . . . nine. Ashara . . . ten.

Ten donkeys, Baba. Have a good trip!"

| خمسة | أربعة | ثلاثة | إثنان | واحد |
|---|---|---|---|---|
| Khamsa | Arba'a | Thalatha | Ithnan | Wahid |
| 5 ٥ | 4 ٤ | 3 ٣ | 2 ٢ | 1 ١ |

Over the sandhills,
through sandy valleys.
A long, long way to the market.

6

"Ten donkeys
going to market.
I am a lucky man!"

7

"Ten donkeys . . .
going to . . . WAIT!

Wahid . . . that's one.
Ithnan . . . two.
Thalatha . . . three.
Arba'a . . . four.
Khamsa . . . five
Sitta . . . six.
Sab'a . . . seven.
Thamanya . . . eight.
Tis'a . . . nine. Tis'a! NINE?

A donkey is lost! I am an unlucky man!"

"COUNT AGAIN, JOUHA!"

"Wahid. Ithnan. Thalatha. Arba'a. Khamsa.
Sitta. Sab'a. Thamanya. Tis'a. Ashara—ten!

عشرة
Ashara
10 ١٠

تسعة
Tis'a
9 ٩

ثمانية
Thamanya
8 ٨

سبعة
Sab'a
7 ٧

ستة
Sitta
6 ٦

"The lost donkey is back!
I am a lucky man!"

| خمسة | أربعة | ثلاثة | إثنان | واحد |
|---|---|---|---|---|
| Khamsa | Arba'a | Thalatha | Ithnan | Wahid |
| 5 ٥ | 4 ٤ | 3 ٣ | 2 ٢ | 1 ١ |

"Water ahead. A good place to stop.
My donkeys can rest for a while.

Oh, no—I see NINE!
One ran off again!
I am an unlucky man!"

"COUNT AGAIN, JOUHA."

"I'll get off and count again.

"Wahid . . . one.
Ithnan . . . two.
Thalatha . . . three.
Arba'a . . . four.
Khamsa . . . five.

خمسة
Khamsa
5 ٥

أربعة
Arba'a
4 ٤

ثلاثة
Thalatha
3 ٣

إثنان
Ithnan
2 ٢

واحد
Wahid
1 ١

15

Sitta . . . six.
Sab'a . . . seven.
Thamanya . . . eight.
Tis'a . . . nine.
Ashara! ten!

| عشرة | تسعة | ثمانية | سبعة | ستة |
|------|------|--------|------|-----|
| Ashara | Tis'a | Thamanya | Sab'a | Sitta |
| 10 ١٠ | 9 ٩ | 8 ٨ | 7 ٧ | 6 ٦ |

"The lost donkey came back!
I am a lucky man!"

"Ten donkeys with dates . . . to sell at the market.
I'd better count them again.

Wahid . . . one. Ithnan . . . two.
Thalatha . . . three. Arba'a . . . four.
Khamsa . . . five. Sitta . . . six. Sab'a . . . seven.
Thamanya . . . eight.
Tis'a . . . Tis'a? NINE!

18

"One lost again!
I am an unlucky man."

19

"COUNT AGAIN, JOUHA!"

| ستة | سبعة | ثمانية | تسعة | عشرة |
|---|---|---|---|---|
| Sitta | Sab'a | Thamanya | Tis'a | Ashara |
| 6 ٦ | 7 ٧ | 8 ٨ | 9 ٩ | 10 ١٠ |

"Wahid . . . that's one. Ithnan . . . two. Thalatha . . . three. Arba'a . . . four. Khamsa . . . five. Sitta . . . six. Sab'a . . . seven. Thamanya . . . eight. Tis'a . . . nine. Ashara . . . ten. Ashara! Ten!

The donkey is back! I am a lucky man!"

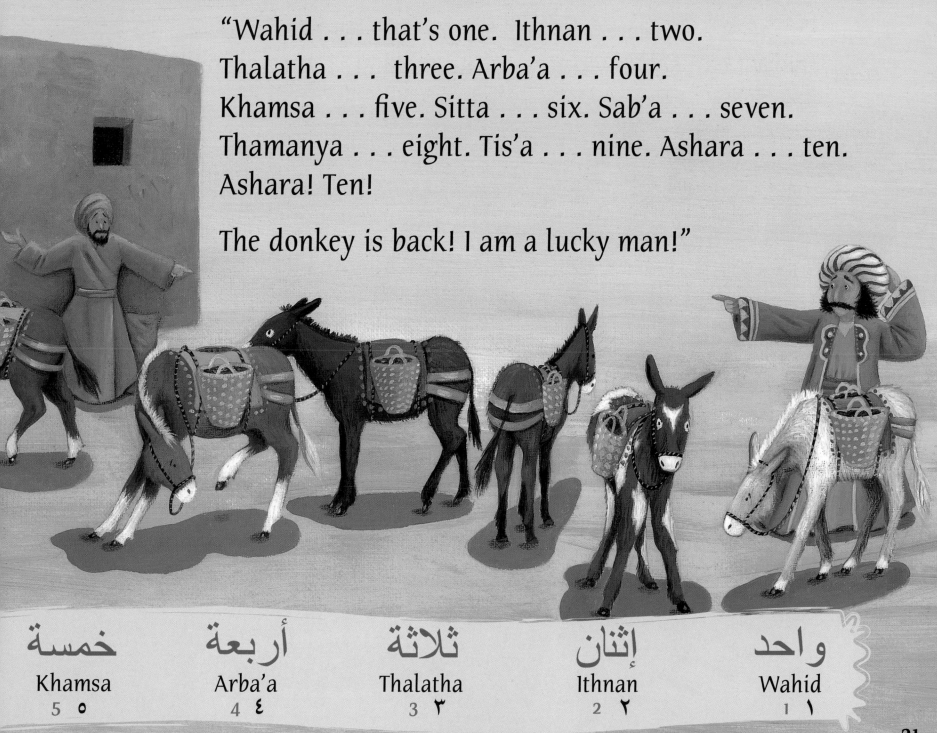

| خمسة | أربعة | ثلاثة | إثنان | واحد |
|---|---|---|---|---|
| Khamsa | Arba'a | Thalatha | Ithnan | Wahid |
| 5  ٥ | 4  ٤ | 3  ٣ | 2  ٢ | 1  ١ |

"Now I can sell my dates at the market. I am a happy man!"

"I won't lose a donkey on my way home.
Now I know what I did wrong.
If I RIDE on a donkey, a donkey escapes!
If I WALK, they cannot run away."

"It's better to walk than to lose a donkey.
I've learned that lesson today."

27

"Almost home! At last I can ride. Oh, no—now a donkey is lost!

Wahid . . . that's one. Ithnan . . . two. Thalatha . . . three. Arba'a . . . four. Khamsa . . . five. Sitta . . . six. Sab'a . . . seven. Thamanya . . . eight. TIS'A! Nine.

"I've come home with just nine. I am an unlucky man!"

"Let me count, Baba." His son helps him count.
"Wahid. Ithnan. Thalatha. Arba'a. Khamsa.
Sitta. Sab'a. Thamanya. Tis'a. Ashara! Ten!

| عشرة | تسعة | ثمانية | سبعة | ستة |
|------|------|--------|------|-----|
| Ashara | Tis'a | Thamanya | Sab'a | Sitta |
| 10 ١٠ | 9 ٩ | 8 ٨ | 7 ٧ | 6 ٦ |

"See, Baba! All here!"

| خمسة | أربعة | ثلاثة | إثنان | واحد |
|---|---|---|---|---|
| Khamsa | Arba'a | Thalatha | Ithnan | Wahid |
| 5 ٥ | 4 ٤ | 3 ٣ | 2 ٢ | 1 ١ |

"A clever son! My lost donkey is found! I am a lucky man!"